Little Pebble™

All Kinds of Weather

Hot Weather

A 4D BOOK

by Sally Lee

PEBBLE
a capstone imprint

Download the Capstone 4D app!

- Ask an adult to download the Capstone 4D app.
- Scan the cover and stars inside the book for additional content.

When you scan a spread, you'll find fun extra stuff to go with this book! You can also find these things on the web at www.capstone4D.com using the password: hot.01891

Little Pebble is published by Pebble
1710 Roe Crest Drive, North Mankato,
Minnesota 56003
www.mycapstone.com

Library of Congress Cataloging-in-Publication Data
is available on the Library of Congress website.

ISBN 978-1-9771-0189-1 (library binding)
ISBN 978-1-9771-0196-9 (paperback)
ISBN 978-1-9771-0202-7 (ebook pdf)

Editorial Credits
Marissa Kirkman, editor; Bobbie Nuytten, designer; Tracy Cummins, media researcher; Kris Wilfahrt, production specialist

Photo Credits
iStockphoto: skynesher, 5; Shutterstock: Daxiao Productions, 19, ER_09, 13, gpointstudio, 9, happystock, 15, Igor Vkv, Design Element, Nepster, 11, Studio 1One, 21, Thaweewong Vichaiururoj, 17, Tom Wang, 1, TXiXinXing, 7, V. Shvd, Cover, wowomnom, 12.

Printed and bound in United States.
PA021

Table of Contents

Whew

I play in the sun.

My skin is damp.

It is hot today!

Why Is It Hot?

The sun heats the earth.

Long days get more sunlight.

They are hotter.

Spring and summer have long days.

They are warm seasons.

The earth tilts toward the sun
in summer.
The sun's rays are strong.
They send more heat.

summer

winter

11

How Is the Weather?

Will today be cloudy

or sunny?

A forecast will tell you.

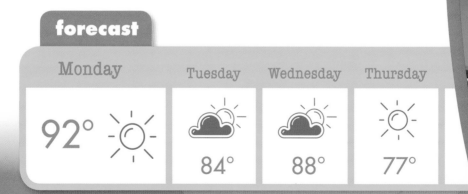

forecast

Monday	Tuesday	Wednesday	Thursday
92°	84°	88°	77°

Clouds hide the sun.

The air feels cooler.

Clear days have more sun.

They feel hotter.

Humid days have moisture in the air.
Your body's sweat does not dry as fast.
You feel hotter.

Whew!

The temperature is high
on a hot day.
Go inside if it gets too hot.

Have Fun!

Hot days can be fun.

Let's play in the pool.

Splash!

Glossary

forecast—a report of future weather conditions

humid—damp or moist

moisture—wetness

ray—a line of light that beams out from something bright

season—one of the four parts of the year; winter, spring, summer, and fall are seasons

sweat—to have salty drops of moisture come out through the pores in your skin

temperature—the measure of how hot or cold something is

tilt—an angle or lean; not straight

Read More

DeWitt, Lynda. *What Will the Weather Be?* Let's-Read-and-Find-Out Science 2. New York: HarperCollins, 2015.

Felix, Rebecca. *What Do People Do in Summer?* Let's Look at Summer. Ann Arbor, Mich.: Cherry Lake Publishing, 2014.

Rustad, Martha E. H. *Today Is a Hot Day.* What Is the Weather Today? North Mankato, Minn.: Capstone Press, 2017.

Internet Sites

Use FactHound to find Internet sites related to this book.

Visit www.facthound.com

Just type in 9781977101891 and go.

Super-cool stuff! Check out projects, games and lots more at **www.capstonekids.com**

Critical Thinking Questions

1. Why are longer days warmer?

2. Why does the air feel cooler on a cloudy day?

3. What happens to your body on a hot day?

Index